Flares

Flares

CHRISTOPHER MERRILL

WHITE PINE PRESS / BUFFALO, NEW YORK

White Pine Press
P.O. Box 236
Buffalo, NY 14201
www.whitepine.org

Publication of this book was supported by public funds from the New York State Council on the Arts, with the support of Governor Andrew M. Cuomo and the New York State Legislature, a State Agency, a grant from the Amazon Literary Partnership, and with the support of the Graduate College and the Office of the Vice President for Research at the University of Iowa.

Printed and bound in the United States of America.

Cover image: Elaine LaMattina

ISBN 978-1-945680-46-5

Library of Congress Control Number: 2020930088

Acknowledgments

I am very grateful to the editors of the following publications, in which many of these poems first appeared: *The American Journal of Poetry, Bengal Lights, The Birmingham Poetry Review, Cloudbank, Connotation Press: An Online Artifact, december, The Enchanting Verses Literary Review, Fulcrum: An Anthology of Poetry and Aesthetics, Härter, Levure Littéraire, Life and Legends, Live Encounters Poetry & Writing, Prairie Schooner, Rattapallax,* and *Transom.*

Thanks, too, to Richard Jackson, who commissioned "The Brooch" for his anthology, *The Heart's Many Doors: American Poets Respond to Metka Krašovec's Images Responding to Emily Dickinson.* San Antonio: Wings Press, 2017; and to Brian Turner, who selected "Genesis" for his anthology, T*he Kiss: Intimacies fom Writers.* New York: W. W. Norton & Company, 2018.

"Notes for a Dance" took shape in Cartagena, Colombia, as part of a collaboration with dancers from the Bebe Miller Company. Boundless gratitude to Bebe for her inspired choreography, to the staff at the U.S. Embassy in Bogotá who arranged our tour, and to the writers who joined me for this cultural diplomacy mission—Emmy Pérez, José Antonio Rodríguez, and Wendy Walters.

Finally, I wish to thank Dennis Maloney and Elaine LaMattina whose steadfast support of my work for nearly three decades has made all the difference.

Flares

Contents

For Tom Sleigh and Jill Staggs

In Petra

I did not hear the Bedouin singing in the cave. Nor did I see the camel gallop off with a Canadian woman who had traveled here to track down her daughter. Nor did I figure that the guard standing at attention before the Treasury would take aim at a group of tourists before a soldier wrestled him to the ground. I stood before three djinn blocks counting my blessings: that the spirit of the place, carved in rose-colored stone, had revealed itself to be a caravan driver who could surely find his way in the dark; that the autumn rains had filled the cisterns, although the granaries were empty; that the bomb-sniffing dogs and sappers under my command had suffered no casualties, unearthing unexploded ordnance from the last war and clearing mines from the new offensive, which was advancing faster than expected. If the decision to pause the operation owed more to supply lines than to tactics, nevertheless I welcomed this time away from headquarters. No more smoke and dust. And all would have been well, if only you had agreed to join me for this journey to the origin—of what? I could not say. But I knew the Bedouin's prayer would haunt me forever.

Lodge

There was no record of our reservation at the hunting lodge, according to the clerk, who somehow managed to find enough rooms to salvage the symposium on nature writing. He was a retired barrister from Jammu and Kashmir, the division of which marked his life, casting light on his offhand manner of identifying the stuffed animals displayed in the lobby—moose and caribou, a tiger, a zebra, a wildebeest. The owner had dropped dead the week before, during a shooting party on the Scottish heath; no one on the staff seemed to mourn his passing. The oldest member of our party, a survivor of the Bataan Death March, liked to say, apropos of nothing, *Now I can live.* Keen to add to his life list, which included raptors from six continents and three separate species of extinct rails, he rose before dawn to walk in the woods, returning for our discussion—which included, at his insistence, the clerk, who was well-read in the literature of his adopted homeland. Their insights colored our exploration of how writers attend to their surroundings. *Now I can live,* said the war veteran, who was in fact on his last legs. How to explain the fever that came over me for you? All I know is that it never broke.

Gothic

The first goat was not named Billy, despite what you may have heard. He called himself Ernest Hemingway, and he spent all day balancing on the top branch of an olive tree, aiming his shotgun at the other goats on the hillside, Che Guevara and Ronald Reagan, who liked to tug his beard when he was in his cups. He would count to a hundred before squeezing the trigger, daring them to bleat again at the church steeple. Che was plotting revolution; the actor could not remember his lines. The sky turned orange, a lightning strike having ignited a fire that charred the mountains and destroyed all the houses and barns in the next valley; a timber baron surveyed the damage from his helicopter, which was running low on fuel; smoke and ash swirled around the olive tree. *Close your eyes,* Ernest Hemingway whispered. *This is going to hurt.*

Explain Yourself

Did God give me a son or a ghost? cried the old woman, peering out the front door. The beggar, who only wanted a handful of rice, hobbled away down the flooding street. The rainy season had begun with a protest march, the statues of the martyrs were blindfolded, and the night watchman, dozing on a hammock strung between two palm trees, wouldn't rouse himself for the wedding guests arriving from the outermost island of the archipelago. *Come on*: these words were painted on the hindquarters of the pig selected for the feast. The old woman feared that her husband, a plodding man, would use a dull knife for the slaughter, creating a bloody mess in the courtyard and bringing more bad luck to a family already singled out for misfortune. Nor was there enough perfume to disguise the fact that the bride was miserable. The beggar took his place on the curb, under a sheet of blue plastic, between a rickshaw and a rabid dog tied to the gate of the Ministry of the Interior. The groom was nowhere to be seen.

After Visiting the Gorky Institute

Someone set fire to the empty boxes stacked behind the shoe store, and the flames spread from the shopping district to the train yard, where three men in fatigues were passing the night trading stories about the strangest things they had eaten as peacekeepers. The smoke didn't alarm them, and they barely registered the fact that they had to raise their voices to be heard above the sirens approaching from every direction. How to compare monkey brains to dog or rat? They stamped their feet as if to keep warm. They toasted those who had not made it home. One recalled losing his passport in Tanzania. Another tried to remember the terms of the Treaty of Perpetual Peace. The third confessed that on his last tour he had hidden in a sheaf of papers taken from his CO's desk the court transcript of a man sentenced to death. He didn't know what had gotten into him. The sky blazed above the tracks, the warehouses, the bridge. A freight train slowed for the curve before the platform, its whistle blowing. Another toast to friendship? Why not.

Venom

Ma salaam, said the martial arts instructor, as if to himself. The shadows lengthened over the heads of his rambunctious students, the mingled odor of sweat and hot tea filled the air, and from the storeroom came the hissing of a king cobra, which had escaped from the zoo. The instructor's terrycloth chafed; his students couldn't wait for class to end. Behind his back they said he had a black belt in cooking rice. Maybe he did. And maybe he could recite the names of all the capitals in the world. But the basic equation of force and counterforce governing his life had not changed, even if the tradition of physical and spiritual practices in the service of self-defense, designed to preserve the cultural heritage of his ancestors, had devolved into a way for the wealthy offspring of local officials to challenge his authority. Meanwhile the zookeeper's frantic search for the snake led him into the alley behind the school, where he paused to calculate how much antivenin the hospital might have on hand. The prospect of catching a cobra terrified him; when he opened the door, listening for its tell-tale growl, he recalled the day long ago, when his fiancée had wakened from a nap to find one coiled on the floor; she bolted out of their flat, never to return. The martial arts instructor promised to name names, if the police closed down his school.

Flare

The rent was late, and nobody thought to dig up the sacks of gold buried under the black flags lining the road through the desert. At dusk a gas flare lit the eyes of a nomad who had lost hope of finding water this late in the season; his herd had been reduced by half, and if he believed the oasis was no longer within walking distance he said nothing to his son, who was planning his escape, not to the city but to the refinery at the edge of the sea. One condition of employment there was to undergo weekly blood tests; the other, to ignore the orders of any engineer who did not kneel before the falconer. *Open the door,* his father said one night in his sleep. *Who is it?* said the boy. *The landlord,* said his father. *His ship sails at dawn.*

Roundabout

As the last wagon of the caravan approached the roundabout, the driver thrashed the horses he had acquired at an oasis hundreds of miles from the former capital; his original team had bolted at the sound of a meteor roaring across the sky at dawn; its glittering remains lit the way to the city. His notes on the drought went on for pages, detailing his losses in a meticulous hand. Some believed his testimony might explain what had propelled their exodus, without hope of alleviating their pain. Loneliness lay on his tongue like dust from a courtyard in the medina, where sheepskins were drying in a wire cage and a laborer recited verses from the Qur'an, rubbing his legs blistered from long days of wading in the vats of the tannery. Who could decipher the graffiti—*New York, New York*—on the palace wall? *Friend or foe?* said a policeman, reaching for his gun. A dog asleep on a sack of cement twitched and whimpered. The horses did not budge. The policeman took aim.

Fall and Recovery

For Jill Staggs

For example, the crack widening in the window of the plane flying over Greenland: *crazing* is the word used by the safety inspector to describe the mesh of lines spreading from the bullet-sized hole in the plastic through which shine glaciers melting in the sea below—ridge upon white ridge gleaming in the sunlight of an autumn morning, which goes on and on as the plane heads westward. The inspector contracts and releases the muscles in his legs, curling his toes under the seat in front of him, raising and lowering his feet, listening, again, to a partita by Bach. Soon it will be time for another meal, another film, and the blue expanse of the sea. The flight seems endless, suspended like a breath above the earth, a line inscribed in the sky subject to the same forces of gravity and velocity that mark the rising tides. The passenger closes his eyes, and as he falls asleep he thinks, *I must be crazy to keep doing this.* The crack opens into light.

In Algiers

The ash fall hasn't reached the city, and yet the sky at noon is pitch-black. Children in the Casbah huddle on the steps, shopkeepers pull down their shutters, and a visiting pensioner from the defeated army scans the crowd outside the cinema for the daughter of the man he persuaded to reveal the hiding place of his best friend. As the water rises in the harbor, a geography teacher sets his basket down and picks through the garbage heaped below the sea wall, wishing he had obeyed his father's order to study medicine. A fisherman, weighing anchor, studies the couples strolling on the beach, under the reproachful gaze of the young man on the boardwalk, who reads too much. Everything—everything!—fires his nerves. The pensioner marches toward the quay, sidestepping a colony of feral cats, which have their eyes on something. *Black and white,* he thinks. *It was all in black and white.* What do the cats see? A dead rat.

Fire

No one had driven the motorbike propped against the stone wall by the chapel since the capture, trial, and execution of the local resistance leaders. The remaining members of the cell fled into the mountains, where late at night they could be heard singing praise songs of their ancestral valor; and since the streams had run dry before summer—the drought was in its third year—they spent their days searching for water; also the keys to the motorbike and the treasury in the chapel, both of which would burn in the forest fire that marked the Dog Days of August—and the advent of the uprising in the capital. Who could have predicted this? Anyone with ears to hear.

On the War Between the States

The bait? A plotline too complex to follow, which we swallowed whole, with predictable results. Around us lay debris from the Rex Ball, where the King was crowned with a plate of bread pudding filched from a wedding reception cobbled together by two families ruined in the aftermath of Hurricane Katrina. They shared a financial advisor, who had persuaded them to stake their future on a match made in Hell—a one-night stand, that is, during spring break in Acapulco; no one was surprised when the marriage was annulled by Easter. Call it variations on a theme from *The Decline of Civilization*. There were so many white faces in the crowd waiting for the last heretic to be burned at the stake that he thought he was in Heaven before the flames reached him. You saw that one coming, didn't you? And yet you refused to leave. Why?

Ivory

Apply yourselves, the nomad told his sons, who were reluctant to drive a parade of elephants over the cliff, despite the booming ivory trade. Rumors flew of a crackdown on poaching, and bounty hunters had arrived from the capital. The prospect of being jailed again ruined whatever pleasure the sons took in their first weeks of freedom, more so when they learned they were suspected not only of ordering an attack on the radio station but of funneling cash to the revolutionaries accused of toppling all the nearby cell towers. They began to fear for their lives after consulting a sorceress, who predicted the elephants would trample them before they could remove the tusks; also that the siren wailing in the distance would grow louder and louder until justice was meted out. *No time like the present,* said their father, winking at them. And he would know, wouldn't he?

The Pastoral Tradition

A man with a red bandana passed the football to the manager of the plantation, who was drawing up plans to grow pineapples instead of sugarcane. A dragon flicked its tongue at a pregnant woman, who could not afford another baby, and so she had gone to the river in search of the ferryman, who had stolen her goat and continued to send her flowers on Sundays. But he was nowhere to be seen. What she found was a jar of eyeballs and ears harvested from the last battle, which had ended inconclusively. And what she remembered of that dark time was dancing a jig, composing in her mind a lullaby for a child fated to be born on the last day of the world. *Sleep, my little mongoose,* she whispered, rooting around in her pocket for a piece of candy. No cobras here. The man with the red bandana cried, *Run!* The manager replied, *This is not a dream.* When the dragon set fire to the dried leaves of a banana tree trampled by an elephant, everyone shouted, *Game over!*

Market Conditions

A consultant from New York drew up a management plan for a plantation on an island in the Indian Ocean, suitable for growing date palms or plantains or the manufacturing of solar panels, all to be staffed by the refugees denied entrance to Australia. The High Commissioner overseeing the temporary camp raised flags from all the countries represented on the island, hoping to stave off a riot, for the living conditions were truly miserable. There was no air conditioning in the blaze of summer, no potable water, insect repellent, or electricity, and nothing to distract the children, who could not stay quiet. They had fled conflicts from across Southeast Asia, entrusting their lives to the captain of a flotilla of creaking boats, who ordered them to toss their belongings overboard. The relief agency refused to ship books to the island, there was no budget for training the men and women in new skills, and every child was sunburned. Would there be a market for what might be produced here? Only time would tell, and it was running out.

The Gold Standard

Our report on the disposition of the shuttered gold mines was overdue, so the Queen sent a courtier to escort us to the gallows, where we watched a coup plotter meet his maker. This was what awaited us if we did not produce by nightfall the exercise in whitewashing commissioned after the palace guard had restored order in the capital. The corpses of slain protesters were burning in the streets, and the sky was thick with flies and dust from the demolition of the opera house; the fat lady would sing no more. Butchers in the open-air market tied yellow ribbons to the soup bones saved for the soldiers confined to their barracks. Peddlers threw oranges at us. What they said about us was true: we lacked conviction; hence our failure to record the number of slag heaps filled with miners who had staked everything on the timely completion of the transcontinental railroad. Nor could we determine the fate of the maid who used the golden spike to sift through the embers in the royal fireplace for the wedding ring cast off in a fit of anger. Tracer bullets lit up the night.

In the Galápagos Islands

The pair of frigate birds that followed the yacht flew so close to the railing around the upper deck that I could almost stroke their bellies. And as they swooped and dipped and climbed I read about Darwin's journey to a salt lake, where the captain of a seal vessel was murdered by his sailors; in the bushes Darwin saw the skull—a fact he recorded with the same equanimity as the temperature, the twenty-six varieties of endemic landbirds that he observed, and the reaction of the lizard he pulled from a hole by its tail. We made landfall on the first day of Holy Week, on an uninhabited island, where a naturalist led us to the top of a volcanic peak, past lava fields and tubes, pausing here and there to explain the difference between parasitic and tuft cones, what happens when lava and gas come into contact with water, how different volcanic slides determined the shape of the island. He pointed out euphorbia, *Tiquilia darwinii* (of the boraginaceae or forget-me-not family), and, when we had returned to the yacht, a blue-footed booby perched on a ledge and three penguins standing on rocks at the edge of the shore. As for the lizard Darwin studied? It stared him in the face, "as much as to say, 'What made you pull my tail?'" A bell rang to call us to lunch.

The Monroe Doctrine

The woman sipping champagne outside the Sherpa hospital did not approve of the speech delivered by the Secretary of State on his tour of Latin America. The newspaper account of its poor reception in the region, where the virtues of the Monroe Doctrine were lost on almost everyone, was what convinced her to take matters into her own hands. She had read it in a café in Kathmandu, where the ex-pat community gathered, and now she stood shoulder to shoulder with political activists and mountain climbers from around the world, marking the tenth anniversary of the King's decision to abolish the monarchy, which coincided with a doomed season on K2—the Savage Mountain. The birth of a new order and a hazy grasp of history inspired her to ask a man with a ponytail to dance the day away with her, and when night fell she took him to her rented flat to hide the artifacts he had discovered on an expedition into the interior—for safekeeping, she told herself. Why not?

The Last Supper

Driven to excess by envy for their illustrious ancestors' achievements in medicine and the arts and despair over their own unrealized ambitions, the thieves slept late day after day. Their failures they blamed on the fires burning in the coast range, dust carried on the wind from deserts in China, fluctuations in the value of the dollar. It was a case history no one would record before the police caught on to them. *Trust your instinct,* they said. *The truth is never the story you tell yourself.* What they mistook for ingenuity was in fact a blueprint for disaster, which their lawyer would call wheels within wheels. The pilot light was out, and yet a flame burned in their hearts. The object of their desire? A diamond left in the vault of a bank about to be reduced to rubble. They cut up their meat in the American way, with the fork in their left hand and the knife in their right, and as they chewed they congratulated themselves on the brilliance of their plan and the riches they would net.

Juice

Not my circus, not my monkeys, said the statistician, ordering the nurse to leave the room in which the cooling body of his brother was surrounded by friends and lovers fated to be cut out of decisions regarding the work that had brought them together in the first place. He explained, in more detail than they could take in, how a client of his, a distributor of canned fruit, had created a market for juices concocted out of what remained in the bins after the harvest—a metaphor for how he would dispose of his brother's unpublished manuscripts. If this resulted in diminished sales of what was already in print he would, of course, reconsider, though he reminded them that a poet's reputation often declined after death. Pomegranates, mangos, grapes, strawberries—mix them together and you have a drink his brother would serve for breakfast. How smooth he was in every social setting. What love he generated in his friends, what light. No accounting for this envy.

Oligarchy

They brought sand from the Gobi Desert, gold from Tashkent, and oil from a tanker listing in the Black Sea—offerings laid on a long table draped with banners of white and red, in a house at the water's edge. They had suspended their studies in hydrology, they told their host, frustrated in their attempts to draw borders for the expanding flood plain; their decision to track him down at his summer place was as inexplicable to him as their determination to walk the length of the Silk Road and the pleasure they seemed to take in detailing their failed experiments. Their inability to describe the motions of an eel forever swimming upstream in their aquarium left him mystified. What did they hope to get for all their trouble? Unlimited funding for their lab and access to the agenda of the next legislative session. The host ordered them to restrict their movements on his property to daylight hours: *If you get too near the pot,* he said, *you'll get dirty.* They wrapped themselves in silks spun in Samarkand, lit a lamp stolen from a flat in Bukhara, sprinkled salt from a cotton field irrigated by the shrinking Aral Sea. The host recalled a childhood outing to a dacha built on the slope above the uranium mine closed after the revolution: how the oligarch let the orphans swim in the pool; how the sky glowed at dusk; how happy they were.

Nomadic

A wide-eyed Gypsy stares out of a barrel sunk into the salt-crusted earth, clutching to his chest a plastic oil container, which he has filled with water; squatting nearby is a kerchiefed woman in a blue floral dress, framed against the white background by three wisps of withered grass, like the points of a triangle, waiting to hand him an empty container, her eyes fixed on something to the right of the photographer. To sow the earth with salt, the traditional punishment for traitors and conquered cities, has in our time inflated the price of greed, with irrigated fields turning white as the cotton grown there in defiance of common sense. Who pays for this? Ordinary men, women, and children: a couple scrambling for water, for example, in a land governed by heedlessness. I bought this postcard in Bukhara, at an exhibit of photographs of the Silk Road. A local writer was giving me a tour of his city, and late in the afternoon we came to a Sufi shrine, which inspired him to tell a story: many centuries ago, a stranger emerged from the desert, promising to save the city from drought. He tapped the earth three times, and then water flowed from a hidden spring, around which the people raised this shrine. We always hope for a miracle.

The Afterlife

The fallen angels huddled by the ramparts of the fortress, debating how and when to scale the walls and what to do if they encountered anyone they knew from their time in the afterlife. Guardianship was much easier than storming the barricades of Satan's foes, and yet they welcomed the challenge of restoring balance to the universe, if only for the duration of the battles they waged, regardless of their outcome. Austerity measures implemented by the Lord of the Underworld had taken a toll on them. Nevertheless they retained their sense of entitlement, which not only informed their tactical and strategic decisions but the timing of their maneuvers. One soldier in the lookout said to another: *The beloved's heart is always breaking. Eyes open.* The angels waited for the sun to rise before they struck another blow against what they would always regard as their better selves.

Excavation

When they lost their passports and the key to the madhouse in Merv, their search for their imprisoned friends grew desperate. A television crew recorded every step of their journey from the observatory atop the library, which displayed in every room a dozen copies of the president's collected writings and a guide to the flora and fauna of Turkmenistan, to an archaeological excavation supervised by a kerchiefed woman, who supplemented her income with carpet-buying expeditions to Istanbul. They stopped at a restaurant to plot their next move, swatting away flies from the rice heaped on their plates, and recalled the national race commemorating the Day of the Horse, when the victorious president, AKA the Protector, crossed the finish line and pitched headfirst into the track. He lay unconscious in the dirt for several minutes before an ambulance arrived to transport him to the hospital. The police confiscated hundreds of cell phones from the hushed crowd and ordered foreign journalists to erase their photographs and video footage—which did not prevent a video of the president's fall from appearing on YouTube. What story would you tell your children about a race that ended in disaster? They were not allowed to leave the country without pledging never to reveal their suspicion that their friends' remains were buried under a golden statue of the president riding a horse. Nor were they permitted to comment on the new honorary title bestowed on him: *The People's Horse Breeder.* The chief archaeologist set her sights on Lake Baikal, where it is said that Christ exclaimed, *Beyond this there is nothing*—which is why corn does not grow there. Rusting fishing boats lay in the sand far from the shore, like camels.

The Final Act

With a snake looped around her neck, the acrobat leaped from the high platform into a cloud of incense swirling in the aerial hoop from which she would swing in the circular flight pattern of a bird in the cave painting discovered just before the war. The incense rose from a table at the edge of the ring, behind which the ringmaster summoned clowns and jugglers at regular intervals so that he could go feed the lion in its cage. A priest tracked the aerialist's movements through the dark, as if to monitor the changes roiling his own soul, which he likened to a wheel of flames spinning under the big tent. The circus would leave town in the morning, never to return, and the priest was not alone in his contemplation of last things. The snake began to constrict the performer, who grew confused, her rotations slowing, and now she was unable to remember where she was in her routine. The priest mumbled a prayer for the ringmaster, who shook the censer like a whip. The lion roared once then lay back down. The crowd yearned to fly away.

From the Archives

For Barry Sanders

He was a curator at the Museum of Desire—although his training was in the history of the book, illuminated manuscripts exciting him more than most erotica. And perhaps because he could no longer muster any enthusiasm for his work he explored the archives with a degree of detachment that inspired envy among his younger colleagues and silent derision from his assistant. Thus it was that one morning, while searching for receipts from an exhibit on the mating habits of a tribe but lately discovered in the Amazon, he found a photograph from a masquerade ball at which the most beautiful actress of the day had dressed up as an ornithologist armed with a shotgun. She was posing before a golden cage in which perched a passenger pigeon stuffed by the founder of the museum, and there was something in her expression—a lift of her brow, a glint in her eye—that told him she would shoot the host after the guests left. The crime remained unsolved—the actress had an airtight alibi, courtesy of a paramour who had returned that night from an expedition to the rain forest—and soon it was forgotten by all but some amateur sleuths, a motley assortment of zealots who refused to circulate their findings. Nor was there any mention of it in the history of the museum, an omission for which the curator could blame no one but himself. Years passed; and if on her deathbed the actress muttered something, which one nurse interpreted as a confession and another as a plea for mercy, she went to her grave considered by most to be an icon of the silver screen. There was nothing to do but display her photograph in the front foyer of the museum. The curator's assistant could not contain his fury.

Sin Spots

The solar storm took the satellites by surprise; also the faithful repenting for their sins. It was the season of renewal, with temperatures hovering near freezing and the rain turning to sleet. No one on the block could figure out how to assemble the furniture delivered in boxes overnight. We blamed our failure to foresee the tragedy on sunspots, which the former chief of staff heard as *sin spots*. He was making the rounds of talk shows to atone for his role in leading the country into a war destined to end in defeat. It was not his fault, strictly speaking, that the military planners had ignored his questions— which he had been reluctant to raise. He had better things to do: replace the cheesecloth in the wooden cider press, for example, or sand the planks of wood set aside for the fence around the cemetery. So much to do! The sky throbbed in red and green and blue. The needle on his compass spun around, like the body of the dictator hanged at dawn—a man he once called his friend. Put the bookshelf here. No. There.

The Stage

They built a dance stage in Phnom Penh with wood imported from the Mekong delta, nails forged with a mallet taken from the killing fields, and music composed for a troupe that waited too long to flee. The defense attorneys for the former Khmer Rouge official convicted of ordering a mass killing during the evacuation of the capital planned to file the paperwork for an appeal before the rainy season; the rest of his convictions for crimes against humanity, each of which carried a life sentence, he would not contest. The translation of the *Black Notebooks* was taking longer than anyone expected— except for the philosopher, who covered his tracks with the care of a jewel thief commissioned to write his life story without revealing the secrets of his trade. *Too late*, the guard said when the judge ordered him to remove the prisoner from the general population. That convoy left at sunset, crossing the border before the curtain rose.

Without

On the first day the goat climbed to the top branch of the acacia tree and said, *The ship sailing to the new world will sink before it leaves the harbor.* He stayed there all night, counting the stars in three constellations he had never seen before, and in the morning he rinsed his face, saying, *The fishermen mending their nets will never take to sea again.* Leaves fell from the tree, the herder called from the ridge, and the goat, frisky in the heat, bounced on the bare branch until late afternoon, when he drifted off to sleep, unafraid of what the waxing moon might bring. That night he dreamed of a hyena chasing a lion up a valley into which the sea rushed, dividing the continent between the ones with gold and the ones without. And when he woke at sunrise on the third day, believing the whitecaps in his dream were the pages of an unwritten book left on the ridge from which the herder called to him, he said, *Here I am.*

Voltage

That night a circuit breaker was tripped in the power plant by the sea, a red light flickered atop the tower on the ridge, and a band of soldiers from the capital halted their advance on the rebel stronghold. They passed around cigarettes; rechecked their orders and coordinates; decided it was too late to switch sides. Fanning out across the road, ruing their allegiance to a corrupt regime, they waited in dread for the command to resume their march to the fortress, which they had visited on a school trip. The leader of the insurgents used to work there as a docent, and for the children the highlight of his tour was the reenactment of a medieval battle, with men bearing armor and weapons collected from every corner of the realm—broadswords and battle axes, crossbows and catapults, gauntlets and great helms. It was said that in preparation for the revolt the docent had steeped himself in the history of siege warfare to learn what would break the will of the invaders and bolster the spirits of the besieged. The tower's warning light reminded one soldier of seeing Mars for the first time through his father's telescope. If only he had heeded his advice to study abroad! The electric line above him hummed.

The Orchard

They waited in the orchard for the order to advance on the farmhouse from which the rebels had long since fled. No one knew what had become of the informant whose tip about a meeting of the insurgency's leadership had led the soldiers to cordon off a village that did not appear on any map. He was a vintner recruited after the invasion, skilled in the art of adaptation, and if he compared intelligence gathering to harvesting his neighbor's grapes, a pleasant diversion for an old man, he also told his paymasters that fermentation carried risks—a warning they dismissed as drunken talk. The wind died, swallows dipped and soared around the trees, and in the noonday heat the soldiers drowsed or dreamed of women they would have on their next leave. The new lieutenant was revising his plans for graduate school, when a peach landed on his backpack. He jumped to his feet, folded and unfolded his map, ordered his men to look sharp. A sniper took up his position on the ridge. What had the vintner said? *Ripeness is all.*

The Festival

The ceremony is over, said the disgraced poet before he was led to the wall above the holy lake. His prophesies about the revolution had not come true; he had misread the hand-lettered signs of the protesters in the square; and from exile he had pronounced his best friend dead of snakebite, despite the fact that anti-venom serum had in accordance with tradition been administered after evening prayers. But he was handed a substantial check, an orchestra played music from his war-torn homeland, and although no one clapped when he was presented with the golden antelope he still smiled for the cameras. There he stood under the plaque of Anna Akhmatova, dispensing wisdom to the international journalists bussed to the event, while the crowd wandered off to lunch or to look at the statues of figures, historical and mythological, who had created new civilizations—Genghis Khan, a goddess from the Ramayana, a pair of Russian saints, an African chief. Bright sunshine. Yellow fields of mustard covering the hills. Two hydrofoils circled the lake every two minutes. Pennants—blue and white and red and green and orange—imprinted with sutras fluttered in the wind. *Beware of the well,* the poet said enigmatically. The journalists wondered if the translation was correct. A hand was raised. *Can you repeat what you said?* The poet shook his head.

The Brooch

After a print by Metka Krašovec

The jeweler waved her soldering iron like a baton, scattering drops of silver on the wall, the floor, and the old dog, which started from sleep, whimpering, and scampered around the studio, stopping every step or two to lick its tail. Anyone could see she had selected the wrong gems for the brooch commissioned to appease a woman who had not imagined her husband capable of infidelity. Yet she was determined to please her client, aligning her memory of a winter afternoon with him during the siege, in a walkup overlooking the river that no longer froze, with his desire to repair a broken marriage. How they giggled under the covers about the name she had bestowed on the dog abandoned by its owner: *Obscure.* The deadline for delivery was the anniversary of the end of the war, which marked the midpoint of their affair. On the bill of sale she called the brooch *The Dying Eye.* When she blew out the candle on her table, the dog howled at the silver stream pouring through the window, fusing the future to the past. This was music to her ears.

The Fish Market in Guangzhou

A boy hoists a plastic bag of frogs onto a wooden pallet, baby eels slither around a white pail, and sea snakes curl under and over one another, venomous phrases traded at the end of the day. The pigeons netted overnight coo in the cage left in the road. Turtles on the endangered list withdraw into themselves, while shirtless men haul blocks of ice from a truck parked in a pothole. Where rainwater pools in an alley the guide stops to rehearse the history of the market that overlooks the river—fishermen and families and faith. She doubts the Ministry of Culture will reverse or explain its decision to cancel the festival at the last minute. Nor will the actors, dancers, and musicians be reimbursed for their expenses or compensated for the time lost to preparation and travel. *Bu fang bian,* she tells the performers. *Not convenient.* No sharks or rays in the aquarium, no storyline for the visitors who cannot change their flights—and no way out of here.

Mirrors

Monuments to folly lined the severed arteries on both sides of the divide, and while the surviving children in the South played under the bleeding icons until nightfall, their counterparts in the North puzzled over the script in the books they inherited. The mirrors stacked against the wall cracked when a wave rippled around the earth, baffling seismologists, and the reflections of the streetlight shimmered through the long night of the winter solstice. How did the Green Line become a nurse log for a grove of lemon trees? The fruit lay all around the bus, which would not release the tourists until daybreak, when the street sweepers knotted their neckties before inviting the domestic workers arriving from abroad to the community center dance.

Stew

The widow removed from the stove a saucepan of rabbit stew, which she had prepared on the morning of the fire then set aside when the owner of the garment factory knocked on her door to deliver the news, tragic, if unsurprising, that her husband was to blame for the disaster. He was an insatiable womanizer who had betrayed her from the first days of their marriage; her tears at his funeral, which drew a handful of people, signaled relief more than pain. She stirred the stew, adding thyme and oregano, relishing the fact that the pressure not to antagonize him had dissolved in the smoke that shrouded the city for three days until rain sweeping in from the coast cleared the air. What remained was the desire to gaze out the kitchen window at the mountains in the distance, where long ago she had spent the night with a man she would never see again. She ladled the stew into her husband's bowl and sat down to eat.

Faith

The brick that fell from the scaffolding around the cathedral, the foreman having ordered his men to make room for the sandblasters, landed between a man and a woman whose argument had escalated into a shouting match. He had raised his hand to wave off everything that had gone wrong in the last year (the things he said to her in anger, the pattern of his business partner's lies, the consequences of his mother's failing memory), and she had stepped away—which saved her life. They stopped in their tracks to stare at the brick dust and the hole in the sidewalk. In the morning sky, a fingernail of moon hung above the shrine on the mountaintop. No rain in the forecast. Nothing to do but turn to each other, and say, *God is good.*

The Wedding

No use pretending anymore: the storm that moved in overnight, pelting the city with rain and hail, changed nothing for the doorman, who could not pay for his daughter's wedding. His threat to reveal the bridegroom's secret before the bachelor party had fallen on deaf ears, and now he had no walking-around money to distribute to the canvassers shepherding voters to the polling booths in the basement of the church, where old women were putting the final touches on the preparations for the reception. The reservoir was full, a crack appeared in the dam, and when it gave way, releasing a wall of water that flooded the village, the doorman locked the church, refusing to let anyone in or out. It was time to count the votes. No one could predict the results of the election, which might or might not reflect the will of the people. *To have and to hold from this day forward,* he whispered, *for better, for worse, for richer, for poorer, in sickness and in health. . .*

Home

First we tore up the floorboards, searching for the deed to the house, which had come into our possession as a result of an intricate and perhaps dubious legal process. Then we hollowed out some of the beams in the foundation: nothing. Behind a cushion in the living room was a leather-bound hymnal containing music we didn't recognize. Termites had eaten through the woodpile; the names and dates on the gravestones in the family plot were illegible; grief insinuated itself into the fabric of our search. We needed a new vocabulary to describe how sunlight on the dying spruces upset the balance we had achieved in our relationship to nature—and one another. Thus a woman who professed to dislike violence became enraged at the sight of green, while a man known for his diplomatic skills grew so brittle that changes in the weather left him bedridden. Of the family we guessed that when they were little someone had braided the hair of the girls, who moved away after the foreclosure. No trace of their parents, who were carried by the currents of desire to separate cities. We might never clear the title to this land.

Paprika

In memory of James Tate

The dining room table was set with china and silverware I had never seen before. "I made your mother's chicken divan," she said. "But I'm a vegetarian," I said, "and my mother died before we were married. Where did you find her recipe?" She turned down the lights, lit a candle, and dipped a ladle in the casserole. "On your hard drive," she said, "before you changed your password." I turned my plate over to examine the figure of crossed swords worked into the porcelain, wondering when we had acquired such exquisite Meissen ware. An Igbo proverb came to mind: "The frog doesn't hop in the afternoon unless it is being chased." "What are you trying to tell me?" she said. Against my better judgment, I tasted her chicken divan. "Something's missing," I said. "One hand cannot wash itself," she said, quoting my mother for the first time ever. "Did you write a check for $40?" I said. "It's the cost of a new mailbox key," she said. "Paprika," I said. "It needs paprika."

From the Memory Ward

I am calling to report a missing person, my mother said. Suzanne Seigman France escaped from Greystone in 1971, disguised as a volunteer from the Mental Health Association; no one has seen her since. She was determined to track down her husband's mistress, Amelia or Emily, who was a secretary at the record company to which he made a series of bad loans, any one of which could have cost him his job. Ignore the court's stipulation that he left the bank of his own accord. Nor can you hold her responsible for failing to notice that her milk dried up after her son was born: he was never going to be very strong anyway. And now it falls to him to record what I can remember of her life on the run: every night in a new hotel. Bless him.

Elevator

What the rat hears at night, she whispered to the colleague who accosted her when she was waiting for the elevator. *What the bird hears in daylight*, he replied when the doors opened. The tourists inside, laden with shopping bags and umbrellas borrowed from a hotel on the other side of town, heard nothing, she decided, pushing the button for the lobby, while he regarded them as reflections in a chain of mirrors, the breaking of which could doom the planet to decades of bad luck. She figured they had wandered into this building in search of the restaurant on the top floor, which the health department had closed down months before; he thought they had come to see the bullet hole in the bar from the shootout between the police and a government official later charged with fraud, although the bar would not open until five. All at once the elevator stopped, between the thirteenth and fourteenth floors, and in the ensuing silence, which grew more uncomfortable as the minutes passed, she thought, *What the rat hears at night.* He almost said, *What the bird hears in daylight.* The tourists stared at one another until the elevator began to move.

The Rise

"Be passersby." The Gospel of Thomas, 42

They didn't notice the flour spilling from the woman's jar. For this stretch of the road had been the scene of a fierce battle between rival militias; what caught their attention were the coins, bullet casings, and charred identity papers heaped on the rise on which the prisoners were shot. Sunlight glinted off the coils of wire, which some believed would never rust. Smoke and dust on the wind. The scribe took notes on everything the guide said: the acreage of the vineyard spreading to the mountains; the age of the olive trees obscuring the view of the sea; the number of civilian casualties. He planned to collect these veiled sayings into a book titled *In the Realm of the Fallen*, which would not be read for centuries. The woman? She flung the broken handle of the jar into the ditch beside the road, and fell to her knees, beaming.

On Gnosticism

Kit's song was a lesson plan for the gutless—the posse of pickpockets who held us hostage for the duration of the Festival of Roses. The boss said a ghost was wreaking havoc with our excavation of the site chosen for the new Costco, and who were we to contradict his economic rationale? We lacked evidence and the wherewithal to challenge the archaeologist who unearthed a scroll an ocean away from the cave in which a wandering ascetic had secreted it. *Stick to what you know,* said our boss—which was that he was often sauced by noon. Kit thought he had nothing to fear for arguing that a rising tide lifts all boats. He was wrong. The caustic music teacher baked into her exercises in counterpoint hatred for every race but her own. Kit loved her more than he could say. After we were released, he went to look for her in the haystack, where the pickpockets had hidden their loot. *All matter is evil,* he sang. All he needed to start a war was a match.

Cheddar Gorge

The incinerator in the garden was going full blast. The doctor fed the flames with his records, which dated back to the war, lest his children learn which patients had not paid their bills—dairy farmers, policemen, an insurance salesman, a mechanic, the postman, the choir director, the bank president whose delinquent son had a history of trouble. The doctor knew his children would not take into consideration the nature of his relationship with the sick and dying, who filled his freezer with cheese. Nor did he still dream of visiting the limestone caves in Cheddar Gorge, where vintage cheddars matured for a year or more by an excavation that yielded Britain's oldest human skeleton, Cheddar Man, who lived 9,000 years ago; the hole in his head suggests he met a violent end, perhaps at the hands of cannibals, who fashioned skulls into drinking cups. What cannot be stored underground or burned? The real reason why his wife was at church deciding on the music for his funeral. Ashes swirled in the wind, darkening the sky before settling on the bed of miniature roses, where he had buried fetuses until the authorities found him out. He could taste the mustard spread on a cracker topped with a slice of cheddar, which each night he would wash down with a beer. *This is the life,* he liked to say when the last patient was gone.

Inventory

When he took stock on the last day of summer, tallying the security costs of his deputy's leaks to the press, the scale of the dry-docking operation brought on by a storm upgraded to a hurricane, and the likelihood of his being reappointed to a commission established for the sole purpose of postponing reforms in any sector, his legendary optimism faded; also his faith that the box of rough diamonds locked in his safe would ease his legal troubles if his staff betrayed him. Success had warped his view of the risks inherent in trusting women who were underpaid and men who did not like to work. But if the equinox was not the time to make amends? No wind, no clouds, nothing. The harbor was still empty. He could not catch his breath.

The Bench

Today I saw two tractor-trailers parked at the end of the road, in the tumbleweeds above the wash into which the runoff had carried brush, bottles, and the mattress of a homeless man found in the arroyo, after the first snow. Yesterday my friend said she had to lay off her entire staff, and then at a yard sale she paid for a bench carved by a Native American in the nineteenth-century, which was worth ten thousand dollars; it didn't fit through her door. At the same time a well-known novelist wanted her to return the love letters he had written to her when she was a student, while the divorced Hungarian renting her house in the Yucatan had changed the locks on the doors so that the caretaker couldn't interrupt his afternoon lovemaking. For some reason this reminded me of the time an old woman sat in a chair by the pool, waiting, perhaps, for us to bring her a plate of food. The sun was setting on the mesa, which most of our guests were climbing before dessert. A writer said, "Old Mother Ray, do you think she knows how to spell the word *fuck?*" Lately I have been thinking about the failure of my marriage: how I cannot face the prospect of spending another night alone; how I lack the wherewithal to leave. Here's what I saw today: a thick patch of ice under the eaves of the hotel; sunlight gleaming off a road sign; a hangnail on my little toe; a torn packet of sugar fluttering to the floor of the dining hall; a man in prayer by the arroyo; a silver barrel half-buried in the sand, capped with a golden cage in the shape of a dervish's hat: my heart.

Two-Star Hotel

The ceiling caved in on the night of the new moon, trapping a guest from Malta, a hunchbacked man who had to wade through the debris in his pajamas, and the receptionist listening at the door of a couple who had not left their room for two days. The receptionist came from the desert, like the couple, and if she was reluctant to carry out the local security official's latest orders still she had laid aside her scruples and her annotated copy of *The Interpretation of Dreams* to download the hard drive from the laptop in their safe. Now she lay on the floor, covered with plaster, moaning, her legs shattered, while the couple, exhausted not from lovemaking but from the resolution of a long-standing argument, slept on. They had taken a difficult decision, the consequences of which might not become apparent for some time. *Skin for skin,* he had said to his sleeping wife before rising to dress in the dark, to leave for good—and then, inexplicably, he had returned to her side... Prayer flags hung from the hedge around the house in which monks were hiding, bearing messages for the herder to bring over the mountains to the government in exile. An old man carrying pails of steamed rice across the courtyard paused to adjust the pole on his shoulders. The woman circling the dung-heap did not lift her eyes at the sound of something new—the crack of the earth opening in the orchard untended since the war. The drunkard under the acacia tree muttered in his sleep, *I alone escaped...* The couple did not stir.

Providence

The remains of a sunken ship, in the harbor at sunset, silenced the rowers. They lifted their oars to gaze at the charred timbers jutting from the water, and as their boat glided around the stern of what was once a barge, a freighter, or a fishing trawler they heard the cry of gulls, a creaking buoy, traffic on the bridge. Their foray upriver was behind them—the hurricane barrier, the unlit lamps, the kindling banked for the bonfires of the festival... The coxswain stood up to survey the wreckage. Was it burned or abandoned? He could not tell. The wind stirred the turbines across the bay, where bilge poured from a container ship docking overnight. One rower wondered why the outcasts settled here. "Liberty of conscience," said another. "Land," said a third. "And trade." The new assisted living center came into view. A mink in the cattails along the shore slid into the water. The coxswain took his seat. "Ready all," he said. The team leaned forward. "Row."

Ritual

Tickle me, she said to start the day. It was the first thing she remembered saying to her father, who tickled her awake until she was ten years old. He was long gone by the time she learned to please her lovers with this request; and when she slept alone, which was more often the case now than not, she said it louder, as if to test her voice. She understood why it is impossible to tickle oneself—how the brain responds only to the unexpected—and still she hoped for surprise, lightly touching the soles of her feet, the backs of her knees, her underarms. She kicked away her down comforter, raised her sheet to let it float down onto her outstretched body, gazed out the window. The mulberry tree was in blossom, the sky had not clouded over. She checked the clock. There was still time to catch a train to the city, time to call someone out of the blue.

The Crisis

For Yiorgos Chouliaras

Everyone talked about the crisis—unemployment, illegal immigrants, German perfidy, graffiti on all the walls. Yet the cafés were full, flowers bloomed in pots on the balconies, and in the new archaeological museum men lectured their children on the history of the Greeks—war, occupation, brave deeds, politics, thievery—and the tragedy of the Elgin Marbles, reproductions of which ribboned the walls. My friend said that on his way to a poetry reading he had asked the taxi driver if he could smoke; when he had finished he went to throw his cigarette out the window. The driver offered his hand instead, instructing him to crush it in his callused palm, for he had been a baker. *The crisis*, the driver said, *is nothing compared to what I have suffered.* He had a family, a bakery, a shop, a restaurant. Then his wife began to sleep with other men—in his own shop! No one in the village came to his defense. So he moved to Athens, losing hundreds of thousands of Euros. My friend made light of his own problems—another divorce, an eye operation, aging relatives. *The crisis*, the driver said, *it is nothing. Do you hear me? Nothing.*

Auld Lang Syne

Estranged from his family, the broker sat with a beggar at the edge of the cliff, debating the merits of the proposed changes to the tax code and the likelihood of the king accepting the resignation of his general counsel. He stirred the embers of the fire, determined to keep it burning until daybreak, when he would have to decide whether to return home or hurl himself into the abyss. How to undo what cannot be undone, redeem the unredeemable? The first incision he made in the cemetery, on the last day of the mourning period for his mother, hurt less than he had expected, which led him to delay breaking off the love affair that was undermining his position at the firm until it was too late. What had his father told him last New Year's Eve? *Beggars can't be choosers.* His ignorance of his fiduciary responsibilities had astounded the general counsel. Ground Zero would assume new coordinates for both by the time the sun rose over the mountains.

Dead Letter

The recruit marched through the woods, certain he could smell smoke, although the sky was clear save for the contrail of a jet fighter flying toward the front line of a battle—which historians would call the largest bloodbath of the war. The leather straps of his rucksack rubbed his shoulders raw, and as his blistered heels bled in his wet boots his anger mounted over the lieutenant's order to wade through a marsh, exposing him to sniper fire and mortar shells until he caught up with his fellow soldiers, who were resting in the woods. Why he had forgotten or neglected to write a final letter to his beloved, which would be delivered to her upon his death, was a question he could not answer. For the smoke flaring in his nostrils was the last message he would ever receive, a blank page opening before his eyes. *My love,* he might have begun, *I am always thinking only of you. . .*

The Word

The message was ambiguous: *I hope your language has arrived in Harare.* But on the drive from the airport into the capital, as phrases began to take shape in my mind (*soldiers standing in the back of a pickup truck, an avenue of jacarandas in blossom, the high white wall around the State House*), it became clear to me that I might search for weeks, at the edge of sleep, in books and museums, in cafés and alleys, and still not hear a word true enough to serve as the cornerstone for the structure I must build, in poetry or prose, to house the guest who never leaves. Indeed he was waiting for me in the lobby of the hotel, dressed in my grandfather's morning suit. He didn't speak—he never speaks—and pretended not to notice me. I gave my passport to the clerk, signed the register with a flourish, and went to my room, which opened onto the courtyard. The tables were filled with government officials, businessmen from South Africa, families on vacation. I had no hot water or towels; the lock on my safe was broken. No doubt he was waiting for me in the bar, and so I rehearsed my speech: *Welcome. May I show you to your room?*

In Unison

The bell hanging supervisor did not show up, so the crates were still unopened at dusk, when the last of the worshippers left the tower and the choir of bell ringers, recruited from the Old World, set out for the waterfront in search of the sea captain who had brought them to this God-forsaken land. They checked taverns and rooming houses, brothels and a chapel in which drunken sailors sometimes slept. The ship had not left the harbor, which was small comfort to the men renowned for the changes they could ring, standing in a circle under a belfry, pulling one rope after another in their white robes, clockwise, tick tock, tick tock, the bells swinging up and down, thousands of changes rung on the heavy air, sounding in the streets of a city they might never see again. They found the supervisor hiding in an alley, his pockets stuffed with silver, a litter of kittens mewling in the canvas bag slung over his shoulder. *Sing for us*, they demanded—and he did.

Translation (I)

Oscula—this was the word on the tip of the tongue of the woman who refused to travel further down the coast without assurances that she could film whatever she liked. The soldiers patrolling the beach were negotiating the terms of their surrender to the insurgents, who had invited her to join them for the march to the capital, and she was surprised by the mixture of emotions she felt at the prospect of peace. The enticements of the sun and sea were parceled out among the families gathered on the shore, the fishermen lining the jetty, and the feverish man pulling a barrel full of monkeys down the boardwalk. He stopped to wipe his brow and saw, riding at anchor in the harbor, a ghost ship laden with medicine and provisions. There was an old man collecting coils of rope in the wrack and rocks below the hotel, which had been attacked on the first day of the war. How it remained open throughout the siege was a mystery to everyone but the manager, who cautioned guests not to leave their satchels under the table, or else they would lose their money. Wiggle your hips, throw something out—it was all the same to him. Diamonds vanished from the market, and no one seemed to mind. The soldiers laid down their weapons and removed their boots, posing for the camera. *Kiss me*, the woman said, remembering—and they did.

Translation (2)

The word was on the tip of his tongue when a bird flew into the picture window and fell into the bushes, twitching in the setting sun. He could hear his mother, dead these many years, ordering him to make his bed—and not to roll his eyes when she talked to him. Smoke rose from the mill beyond the last row of sugarcane, where a peasant had hacked the head off an Egyptian cobra. The man took down from his shelf a field guide, watching the bird struggle to its feet. Perhaps it was a river warbler, migrating—where? When it flapped its wings, he said, *Exactly. Right?*

The Zoo

His parachute failed to open; also his reserve chute. And his instructor was on the plane banking toward the Rio Grande, returning to the landing strip on the mesa, where they had met in the spring. A man in a free fall, spread-eagle on a cushion of air between two mountain ranges, is not a metaphor for anything beyond the fact that things end, sometimes spectacularly. This he had known since summer, when she had warned him that it could not continue like this, and now on a cool autumn morning the diver had never seen such a rush of colors: the cerulean sky; the red soil with which his wife threw pots for the craft shows; the green of the piñon pines. There was smoke on the wind from a burning field, flecks of blue sparkled in the brown river, and he could almost taste the juniper berries about to be plucked by the magpies. His life did not flash before his eyes as he plummeted toward the earth, his arms flailing like a swimmer dragged out to sea. What came to him instead was a moment in the kitchen with his mother, after a school trip to the zoo. She set out on the table a plate with a peanut-butter sandwich and a glass of cider, lit a cigarette, and said, *Did you see anything interesting?*

Without Objection

The limousine shepherding the actor from the wedding party to the premiere of his film stopped twice—first to pick up a violinist hitchhiking to a music festival, and then to watch a pride of lions devour a zebra they had dragged down close to the national park. Hyenas gathered in a half-circle on the hill above the lions, waiting for them to finish. The film star asked the musician what orchestra excerpts he was working on and where he would audition next. *Don Giovanni, The Magic Flute, The Marriage of Figaro,* he replied, allowing that the Cape Town Philharmonic was his dream. Down the road the warden filled a wheelbarrow with the ivory confiscated from the poacher he had shot dead. Bloodletting was general in those early days of the revolution; also the razing of the churches in which an icon painter had rendered the Harrowing of Hell with exquisite detail. They shot him, too. The violinist recognized none of the films for which the actor had won acclaim on every continent and more than one Academy Award—which seemed to please him. The hyenas were moving in to feed on the scraps. *Drive on,* the actor ordered.

The Concert

The taxi driver seethed, but what to do? He needed the fare. Wayne Newton in a blue-frilled shirt was slumped in the passenger seat, Salman Rushdie pressed his face against the window, and I kept telling my sidekick that no one would believe our luck. The driver pulled his baseball cap down over his eyes, crossing a bridge closed for repairs to avoid the checkpoints on our way out of the city. Wayne's seizure began on a country road lined with birches draped in yellow leaves and didn't end until Salman climbed into the front seat to cradle his head. The driver sped toward the mountains, muttering, *this shall be a sign for you;* the singer, nestled against the novelist's chest, crooned in reply, *that I will visit you for evil.* Deep in the tunnel the driver stopped to let us out at the entrance to the mine shaft, and we descended six stories to an underground stage set up for a concert to benefit the victims of the earthquake. Wayne flashed his badge at the guards, who waved us past a gaggle of reporters waiting for the president. *No one will ever believe this,* I said again, though by now my sidekick was nowhere to be seen.

The Handkerchief

The handkerchief was folded—this was what haunted her long after she had mistaken him for the gardener. He was used to incomprehension, after all, which served as a prelude to his teachings, his forgiveness. Nor was she surprised, despite reports to the contrary, to find the stone rolled away and the tomb empty as the shells they collected by the sea: there was always something elusive about him. She set down her jar of myrrh and asked the gardener if he had taken the body of the one whose promise to return was a window opening onto the dry hills around the occupied city. She thought he had been stolen from her again. She thought the emptiness would never end. The handkerchief once wrapped around his head lay separate from the linen cloths, neatly folded. And when he called her name she turned to Him, crying, *Teacher!*

The Odds

Any fool can read a windsock, monitor sorties along the coast, or counter claims of infallibility made in another language. But it takes patience to devise a strategy to protect those who refuse to lay in supplies before the storm, skill to measure the yield of starlight or radioactive debris from a test conducted in a mine shaft, and genius to predict a couple's future from the length of their courtship. Thus the arrangement of strings dangling from the mirror cracked on their wedding night inspired a bookmaker to give them odds of 25/1. He had stopped taking bets on how far the initials carved in the quaking aspen would stretch before its trunk snapped under snow or slag sliding down the mountain, but he was willing to lay odds on the fate of the targets in the sights of the warplanes circling the city. The cloud cover was so thick that the air controllers could not determine which runway had been spared in the last bombing run. And they feared the test would be repeated until they learned their lesson. *There is no God but God,* said the sheik taping black plastic over the billboard, covering the face of a blonde tennis star whose favorite cream was Clear. It was time to polish the martyrs' names etched in the sidewalk, time to seek shelter. A gale blew from the south. Distribution centers were set up throughout the city, along the coast, and on the road into the mountains. Black letters creaked in the tree: *RIP.*

Genesis

Don't stop, she said as he poured from the watering can the keys to houses she had never visited, drawers she could not unlock, cars reserved for others. Then coins from countries that appeared on none of her itineraries— Ukraine and Indonesia and Iran, not to mention Argentina and Brazil. And hoop earrings she would not be caught dead in, glass beads from a necklace worn by someone else, a silver brooch that made her heart ache. *Don't stop,* she said when there was nothing left—and so he filled the can with water to sprinkle over the objects spread like seeds on the dining room table. One by one they sprouted into new lines of argument, and as they grew she raised her hands above her head, crying, *Don't stop.*

Portage

For Tamera Luzzatto

The canoe had sprung a leak, and so they had to portage to the sea, along a foot path abandoned to marauders from the city. When their guide could not identify the tracks in the mud, the cry of the bird perched in the dead tree behind them, or the markings on the boxcar rusting on the remains of the trestle destroyed in the last war, they set the canoe down and removed from their backpacks the handguns delivered to their rooms the night of their departure. The instructions were clear—*Use only in an emergency*—and yet they could no longer decipher the meaning of the phrase that had inspired them to leave before the ferry sailed into the harbor: *the only anchor ever yet imagined by man.* One fired at the bird, another aimed at the boxcar, the third ordered the guide to take the lead. From the bushes came the sound of something tearing, then footsteps, whimpering, silence. The guide scanned the shore, debating where to put in for the journey to the island on which they would draw up a new judicial code. The bird circled above the tree, and the sea blazed into light. No one knew which way to turn.

The Census

And then the camel spoke: *Where's my makeup?*—a line that provoked no comment from the nomads gathered around the well and no end of mirth among the storks perched in the acacia tree. Its voice was higher than anyone had expected; no one could place the accent. The children laughed when the shepherd appeared at the door to the classroom, clutching a mongoose by the tail. There was red dust on the table and chairs, and hyenas were coming from far away to help with the census. All the carpenters were building abacuses for the ark, which did not amuse the camel. It said, *But the war—is it over yet?* The census-takers lined up at the edge of town, sharpening their pencils. The shepherd pulled from his sack the fangs of a cobra, which inspired the children to roll their beads across the floor. They knew there was no room on the ark for the wounded hyena gnawing at its entrails. How sweet they taste in the noonday sun! *The clouds have put on their mascara*, said the nomads: their cue to resume the march across the desert. The camel snorted, *What was it all about anyway?* No one ever died in that town, according to the records examined by the census-takers, who took turns patrolling the building, fending off the storks and the hyenas. The fangless cobra slithered toward the door.

Meantime

Between the woodpecker's tapping in the topped limb of a dying oak and the arc it engraves, in flight, over the road—over the frost heaves, and chunks of macadam, and cobblestones laid down before the war—and then the garden—the stalks of the dead sunflowers hung with stockings, the wire mesh in which the gourds grew, the footprints in the slush—and finally the tall white gabled house in which the photographer's widow is sorting out the negatives from their last trip together, to the ruins of an ancient city, carved into the side of a mesa overlooking a dry valley, in which they had buried the feather of the bird calling to them (so they had thought in the first days of their marriage) from the beginning of Creation...

Proverbs (I)

You have all you need to kill a snake, said the matriarch, and broke the adder's back with a snap of her wrist, flinging it across the living room into the fire. The children shrieked on cue, to the relief of the director, who was so far over-budget that he feared the bank would call in its loan. Two grips lifted the sofa to set up the next shot, disturbing another snake, which slithered around a coil of electric wire, toward the matriarch, who picked it up and flung it into the flames. *The most beautiful girl gives only what she can,* she declared. One child whispered to the others: *Will she ever let us leave?* The crew voted to go on strike over working conditions. The director threw down his clipboard. *What the wicked dreads will come upon him,* he said. *Wisdom has built her house,* said the matriarch, *she has set up her seven pillars. Better to have a hundred friends than a hundred rubles. Happy in the street, sad in the house. . .*

Proverbs (2)

The sign above the entrance to the mill was unambiguous: *Measure seven times. Cut once.* Inside, Simon Bolivar served coffee to the Buddha, while Genghis Khan fiddled with a samovar hauled from one end of his empire to the other. Water leaked from a vase on the table, pooling by a black cat asleep in a patch of sunlight. The scribe recorded in his notebook a saying new to his ears: *You can't pull fish from the pond without work.* Someone had splashed red paint on the statues in the courtyard of the municipal library; the guards reported almost no reactions among the patrons. Nor did the Buddha dispute his waiter's complaints about his followers being imprisoned in the rhetoric of revolution. The fields were too wet to plow; the soldiers massing in the woods reviewed their orders of engagement; rows of mines planted at the end of the war were ready to bloom. The system of communications created by an arrow fired over the hill occupied by men from the next valley was breaking down. It took the boy so long to learn to talk that his father thought him feeble-minded. In fact he was waiting for the moment to say goodbye. The cat purred. The scribe turned the page and wrote: *That train has left the station.*

Hellbent

For James Galvin

In this direction. Where a miner's drill dissolves in a river of lava, and a pregnant woman wreathed in smoke steps over a crack in the obsidian, and a surveyor who lost his eye to a fishhook squints at the swelling edges of an island in the making. One by one the words take on a luster forbidden to them in the old dispensation, and the earth shines. A volcano rises behind a man and a woman who have lost the gift of small talk. A mourning dove coos in an empress tree until it blossoms. A novice licks his finger, tracing a pool of clear liquid on the shelf to a bulging can of lychees. The abbot says, *We all must die sometime.* The palms beyond the terrace, which block the view of the sea, turn black. The sky spins in this direction. In that.

In the City of K.

The sky blackened. And I was halfway across the square when the heavens opened, with lightning, thunder, sheets of rain. A tram slid off its tracks. A car alarm sounded. Sirens blared by the castle. In the doorway of an antiques shop was a woman smoking, in a white blouse and black pants, framed by gold-lit windows displaying pocket watches, amber bracelets, glassware. When I entered, she said, "You cannot stay here." "But the storm," I said. "It is the rule," she said, ushering me out. I pressed my back against the wall for protection. The street was flooding. The driver of the tram shook his head. Lights flashed from the cameras of the tourists across the way. By now I was completely soaked. The shop girl took a drag. "Thank you," I said. "It is the rule," she repeated.

The Harvest

The shaman dozed on the bench, spent from his exertions the night before, and dreamed he was hanging from a metal hook affixed to the top of the wall surrounding his family compound. He could not explain to the crowd assembling in the street why his punishment had taken this form, because he no longer remembered what crime he had been charged with; his rationale for traveling abroad in defiance of a court order was as mysterious to him as his decision to surrender to a pair of agents from his own government as soon as he had safely crossed the border. Around him apple blossoms fell from a row of trees imported from Bavaria; in the next room of his dream he came to know this extravagant expenditure, disguised in the municipal budget as a gift to the opposition, would bankrupt the city before the fruit ripened. Crows picked up strands of an argument sparked by the burial ceremony he had performed for the goatherd's son—something about the injustice of his decision to begin before everyone arrived. (The train bringing a wedding party to the mountains was delayed.) The ringing in his ears sounded like cicadas waking from their slumber to herald the end of days. No doubt the harvest would be smaller than usual. The shaman did not stir.

Return Visit

The diagnosis was delivered in an offhand manner, in a dream in Dresden, on the vernal equinox: that the cancer undetected in a checkup two weeks before had spread throughout my body. The doctor said my work was complete, and I was given to understand that my family would survive without me. So I left the clinic and drove down a canyon in the Sangre de Cristo Mountains, where I used to hike in the fall, when the aspens were turning gold and there was still a chance. In the sky were all the shades of blue, fitted together like a stained-glass window, which I wanted to savor for as long as possible, with the wind on my face and a magpie squawking from a boulder in the lowering river. I had never felt so happy. The bells were ringing by the brewery.

Notes for a Dance

The trees move into the holding place, eyes open, trunk and leaves, hundreds of poisoned apples scattered over hallowed ground, scrutinized by a flightless bird and all the aunts covering for the woman who slipped away. One story ended, and then another. And then? The moon shone through the plume rising from a volcano. The thief was rolled up in a rug and tossed overboard. Our guide declared a truce. Pause. Eyes closed. Say we were fluent in the language of turn and counterturn, fall and recovery, and then we weren't. Exchange this bag of gold for lessons in the logic of touch, without which each tree stands alone. What can you see, bent double at the waist, but bodies in motion, canoes filling with water, tattoos of flowers on her arms and legs? Eyes everywhere, if you can trust it. Wind equals touch in the cloud canopy: another galaxy to explore.

Stage Presence

The shooting at the wedding party did not begin until daybreak, when the soldiers assembled to sweep the streets, and did not stop until the government fell, when the soldiers laid down their brooms. The widow, hanging her silks to dry from a balcony above the empty square, watched a horse-drawn carriage pass, a bloodied curtain dangling from its window. How to bear the loss of everything she loved with dignity? She lingered in the sunlight, listening for birdsong, bells, the call of the fruit-seller: any trace of the old order. She spread her arms, as if to greet an invisible crowd—elegant men and women in evening attire, rising to their feet. And while her neighbors huddled behind their shutters, monitoring the military broadcasts, she prepared to sing an encore. *Bravo!* cried the soldiers entering the square, trailing clouds of dust. *Bravo!* cried her neighbors.

The Kiss

What did they seek in the storeroom, garden, and bedroom? What drew them night after night to a shuttered house on the bluff above the sea, vowing to repair the damage caused by the shifting earth—cracks in the adobe, loosened tiles in the kitchen? Kiss the feet, the hand, the mouth: this was their credo, adapted from a text translated by an adjunct professor from the valley. *Marry word and deed,* he told them at the final exam. Weeks passed before they got his little joke, by which time he had taken another job out of state. They didn't try to find him: there was too much to do. The rains were heavier than usual, uprooted trees slid down the bluff, and while they debated whether to reinforce the foundation the earth gave way in a wall of mud that covered the road, burying an empty tractor trailer and an armored car returning from the casino. They had no title to the house riding out to sea. The one song they knew had something to do with desire.

Brick

The reddish stubble streaked with birdlime—it's the grizzled beard of a silver miner sleeping off his first strike, his feet propped on a wooden crate behind the saloon, a rope looped in his hands. His aging mule, laden with provisions for winter, gazes at the mountains circling the town, where the rush is on to find new veins, new laws. Someone has stolen the miner's tools and torched his cabin. The flames are spreading, even as a fine mist falls on the valley, carving lines in the miner's brow. He dreams of a canyon too deep to ignore, too dark to follow to its source. Call him a foot soldier in the campaign to wall off access to the sea, the stars. He will not stir until the earth buckles and the buildings heave. Smoke shrouds the mountains, and in his dream of rising waters there is no shore. Vultures are summoned to their nests, bees to the fire, when he sets his jaw, his fingers twitching along the rope. And when the mule stamps its feet, bells ring.

Clay

The *ranchero* galloping toward what he called *the divine contamination of Todos Santos* would not be extradited, even if his horse dropped dead in the plaza. For the *gendarmerie* were patrolling the beach, where tourists would gather at dusk to monitor the nests of sea turtles and the biologists' release of hatchlings into the sea, all under the watchful eyes of coyotes, foxes, crabs, and birds. A potter was removing fired clay from the kiln when a tremor rippled through the courtyard, and the parishioners leaving the church looked at the sky for signs of impending doom only to see the first stars and a cloud sailing past the quarter moon. An expatriate returning from a whale watching expedition scanned the news headlines on his phone then said to his companion: *I see a madman beget madmen.* She was rubbing aloe vera into her sunburned neck and shoulders, contemplating the dinnerware they would pick up on their way home. *We made the right decision,* she replied. *I don't ever want to live there again.* The potter surveyed the damage, listening to the siren wailing by the water. No one could stop that *ranchero.* No one.

Utopia

The cabinetmaker folded his mother's wedding dress and placed it in the trunk, along with a sheaf of love letters to a soldier killed in the Korean War—his father, as it happened, though he had not learned this until the last day of his mother's life. The chaplain had just entered her hospital room when she told her son where to look for the letters that would explain the distance between him and the machinist who had raised him as his son. He remembered the machinist's thick glasses and penchant for making a show out of his son's decision to take up woodworking. Why he left during his wife's final illness would haunt the cabinetmaker until the end of time, like the letters he had memorized before locking the trunk, which he had fashioned with his own hands—a testament not to love or a sense of betrayal but to his belief in fine craftsmanship. The urn containing his mother's ashes he set atop the trunk, beside the globe he spun night after night, convinced that if it stopped at the precise location of his father's death, in the Battle of Heartbreak Ridge, just north of the 38th parallel, a thousand years of peace would reign on earth. Dream on.

Lilacs

What became of the vase of lilacs propped on the windowsill of the house tugged by a truck from one end of the street to the other? The contractor walked underneath the kitchen, confidant the vase would not even tremble when the house was eased into the new foundation, two doors down from the dormitory for the deaf students recruited by the football team. When the church across the street was firebombed on the anniversary of the Night of Long Knives, the students did not stir until the smell of smoke woke them. The marble pieta blackened with soot, and what was singular about the cynicism of the teacher who refused to learn sign language turned plural when the vase went missing. The fragrance of lilacs followed us until our ship sailed out of sight.

The River

The caravan stopped on the bridge to listen to the guitarist, a woman in a yellow sari who had lost her family in a fire set by insurgents. She sat under an umbrella pocked with so many holes that sunlight speckled the fabric saved from her wedding, singing her son's favorite lullaby, trying to remember the dream in which he delivered a lecture in an empty auditorium on the subject of chance, asserting that accident is central to the design of the universe. What did he love? Chocolate, football, and the way the river dried up every summer, stranding the barges carrying grain to the sea. Three days the camels had gone without water. The drivers sang along.

The Author

Christopher Merrill has published six collections of poetry, including *Watch Fire*, for which he received the Lavan Younger Poets Award from the Academy of American Poets; many edited volumes and translations; and six books of nonfiction, among them, *Only the Nails Remain: Scenes from the Balkan Wars*, *Things of the Hidden God: Journey to the Holy Mountain*, and *Self-Portrait with Dogwood*. His writings have been translated into nearly forty languages; his journalism appears widely; and his honors include a Chevalier from the French government in the Order of Arts and Letters and fellowships from the Guggenheim and Ingram Merrill Foundations. He has served on the U.S. National Commission for UNESCO and the National Council on the Humanities; as director of the International Writing Program at the University of Iowa, he has undertaken cultural diplomacy missions to more than fifty countries.

Also by Christopher Merrill

POETRY

Workbook
Fevers & Tides
Watch Fire
Brilliant Water
7 Poets, 4 Days, 1 Poem,
with Marvin Bell, István László Geher,
Ksenia Golubovich, Simone Inguanez, Tomaž Šalamun, and Dean Young
Necessities
Boat
After the Fact: Scripts & Postscripts,
with Marvin Bell

NONFICTION

The Grass of Another Country: A Journey Through the World of Soccer
The Old Bridge: The Third Balkan War and the Age of the Refugee
Only the Nails Remain: Scenes from the Balkan Wars
Things of the Hidden God: Journey to the Holy Mountain
The Tree of the Doves: Ceremony, Expedition, War
Self-Portrait with Dogwood

ESSAYS

The Forest of Speaking Trees: An Essay on Poetry
Your Final Pleasure: An Essay on Reading
Walt Whitman's "Song of Myself" with a Complete Commentary,
with Ed Folsom
"The Million Dead, Too, Summ'd Up":
Walt Whitman's Civil War Writings, A Selection with Commentary,
with Ed Folsom

TRANSLATIONS

Anxious Moments,
prose poems by Aleš Debeljak, with the author
The City and the Child,
poems by Aleš Debeljak, with the author
Even Birds Leave the World: Selected Poems of Ji-woo Huang,
with Won-Chung Kim
Because of the Rain: A Selection of Korean Zen Poems,
with Won-Chung Kim
Scale and Stairs: Selected Poems of Heeduk Ra,
with Won-Chung Kim
Translucency: Selected Poems of Chankyung Sung,
with Won-Chung Kim
The Growth of a Shadow: Selected Poems of Taejoon Moon,
with Won-Chung Kim
The Night of the Cat's Return,
poems by Chanho Song, with Won-Chung Kim
If My Tongue Refuses to Remain in My Mouth
by Sunwoo Kim, with Won-Chung Kim

EDITED WORKS

Outcroppings: John McPhee in the West
The Forgotten Language: Contemporary Poets and Nature
From the Faraway Nearby: Georgia O'Keeffe as Icon,
with Ellen Bradbury
What Will Suffice: Contemporary American Poets on the Art of Poetry,
with Christopher Buckley
The Way to the Salt Marsh: A John Hay Reader
The Four Questions of Melancholy: New and Selected Poems of Tomaž Šalamun
The New Symposium: Poets and Writers on What We Hold in Common,
with Nataša Ďurovičová
Flash Fiction International,
with Robert Shapard and James Thomas
The Same Gate: A Collection of Writings in the Spirit of Rumi,
edited with Nataša Ďurovičová